COOL CAREERS WITHOUT COLLEGE FOR

PEOPLE

WHO LOVE

TO SELL

THINGS

COOL CAREERS WITHOUT COLLEGE FOR
PEOPLE
WHO LOVE
TO SELL
THINGS

**CAROLYN
GARD**

The Rosen Publishing Group, Inc.
New York

Published in 2004 by The Rosen Publishing Group, Inc.
29 East 21st Street, New York, NY 10010

Library of Congress Cataloging-in-Publication Data

Gard, Carolyn.
Cool careers without college for people who love to sell things/ by Carolyn Gard. — 1st ed.
        p. cm. — (Cool careers without college)
Summary: Profiles the characteristics of and qualifications needed for fourteen jobs in various types of sales.
Includes bibliographical references and index.
ISBN 0-8239-3790-9
1. Selling—Vocational guidance—Juvenile literature. [1. Selling—Vocational guidance. 2. Vocational guidance.]
I. Title. II. Series.
HF5438.25.G368 2003
658.85'023—dc21

                                                    2002007453

Manufactured in the United States of America

CONTENTS

INTRODUCTION

If you've ever won the prize for selling the most raffle tickets at school, if you've persuaded others to sponsor you in a charity race, if you've managed to sell your old toys at a garage sale successfully, or if you get along well with others, you might consider a career in sales. In sales, the proven ability to sell things is more important than a college degree. The field is always open to enthusiastic people. Manufacturers and businesses need people to sell products or services as much as they need people to create those products and services.

Going into sales doesn't necessarily mean that you will spend your career standing behind a counter in a retail store at the mall. Most career salespeople started out at the bottom, learning the business from the ground up, but they went on to become supervisors, managers, and store-owners. Some selling careers involve a lot of travel, and some let you be your own boss.

This book describes sales jobs in many different fields and gives you resources where you can get more information if you're interested in pursuing any of the careers. One great thing about a career in sales: You don't need to wait until you graduate to get started. You can go out now and get a part-time sales job after school or on weekends. When you're ready for full-time work, you'll have some experience and contacts under your belt that will make you an attractive candidate for any employer.

1

RETAIL SALES

If you spend your free time at the mall, go out of your way to try new products, and enjoy working with others, retail sales could be a natural career for you. Careers in retail include jobs for cashiers, salespeople, department managers, store managers, dealers, retail buyers, and even business owners.

Anyone wanting to succeed in the retail business must have a genuine liking for people. Retail salespeople help customers find what they need and try to interest the customers in buying the products. A salesperson must have the patience to listen to and assist difficult customers.

Salespeople report to retail managers or sales worker supervisors. Supervisors are involved in all the areas of the store. They are familiar with every aspect of the business, including selling, accounting, advertising, inventory control, and purchasing. They deal with customer complaints that salespeople can't handle. Since retail stores employ a lot of salespeople, the supervisor also makes out work schedules, oversees the staff, and solves any employee problems that arise.

Successful retailers keep up with the trends in their field, whether it is clothing or music or sports. Stores buy their merchandise months ahead of time. When the first cold days of winter arrive, the salespeople have to be thinking about what the customers will be wearing in the spring. Car dealers must decide if their customers will want large vans or sports cars.

A big advantage of the retail sales business is that stores are everywhere. Salespeople are needed in cities, suburbs, and small towns. They work in freestanding stores or in malls. A retail store may be part of a national chain, or it may be a small, family-owned enterprise. A salesperson can

A salesperson and a customer discuss the benefits of a protective vest. People who sell sporting goods should know something about sports and be able to recommend the appropriate gear.

choose to sell what he or she likes—clothes, music, books, sports equipment, and much more. When the salesperson knows and likes the product, that enthusiasm rubs off on the customer and results in a sale.

Education and Training

Many people working in retail started by working part-time in high school and rose to the top by putting in hard work and long hours. Loyalty to a store is often the most important factor in earning a promotion. Even people in the field who have college degrees say that they got their real knowledge from on-the-job training.

National chain stores generally have their own training programs, which may be a combination of classroom work and on-the-job experience. Motor vehicle salespeople have training programs provided by the dealerships. If you work with food, you may need to take a food handler test and be certified by the local health department.

There are some independent training programs you can take on your own to make yourself even more valuable to an employer. Your local school district may offer vocational education courses in retail sales management. Some schools offer certificate programs, which take less than a year to complete. No training substitutes for retail experience, but completing a training program will show your employer that you are serious about the business. That may get you promoted more quickly.

Salary

Salaries vary greatly in this field. The level of responsibility, the years of service, and the size and location of the store all factor into the compensation.

In general, salespeople start out at the federal minimum wage, which was $5.15 an hour as of this printing. When there are more jobs than there are people looking for work, entry-level people may be offered more. The annual salaries of sales managers range from about $21,000 to $37,000. Some workers are paid on commission (a percentage of the sales they make) or on a combination of a salary and commission.

Most stores let their employees buy merchandise at a discount. This can save the employee hundreds of dollars a year. Employees may also participate in profit-sharing plans and receive bonuses and awards for outstanding sales. Salespeople often don't get health benefits or paid vacations, but managers generally do get these benefits.

Outlook

People need products; stores sell those products. That alone makes the outlook good for retail sales. According to the *Occupational Outlook Handbook* published by the U.S. Department of Labor, in 2000 there were about 4.1 million jobs in retail sales. The growth rate of retail jobs is predicted to increase more slowly in the future, but the field has a high turnover rate, which means that new job opportunities are constantly opening up. The opportunities in independent retail stores may decline as competition from national chain stores increases.

A person who has the ability to get along with people, who is excited about the merchandise being offered, who does the homework to keep up with trends, and who is willing to start at the bottom has a great opportunity in retail sales.

The Bad and the Good of Retail Sales

Retail is not a nine-to-five job. Stores are open when the nine-to-fivers aren't working, and that means evenings, weekends, and holidays. On the other hand, employees get days off during the week when the ski slopes aren't as crowded and lines at the bank aren't as long. Salespeople are on their feet all day; if you pursue this kind of work, invest in a couple of pairs of comfortable shoes.

Retail can also be a lot of fun. Every day is new and different. You never know who will come in, how much you'll sell, or what new product you get to highlight.

You can measure your progress by selling more each day and by satisfying more customers.

A shoe salesman helps a customer select a pair of sneakers. Customers expect salespeople to know something about the goods they sell.

FOR MORE INFORMATION

ASSOCIATIONS

National Retail Federation
325 7th Street NW, Suite 1100
Washington, DC 20004
Web site: http://www.nrf.com
The federation offers programs and services in research, education, training, information technology, and government affairs relating to the retail industry.

WEB SITES

Retailer News
http://retailernews.com
This site archives many articles on retail sales.

Retail Industry
http://retailindustry.about.com/cs/jobs
Information on finding retail employment and enhancing your retail job with career information and links to retail recruiters, job boards, industry employment outlooks, and retailer openings.

Retail Sales Worker Supervisors and Managers
http://realvideo.acinet.org/ramgen/49001.rm
Offers a video in RealPlayer format.

What It Takes to Succeed in Retail
http://sales.monsterindia.com/articles/sa_8017
Some down-to-earth suggestions.

Windows on Work
http://www.pbs.org/als/career/retail.htm
Lists and describes retail jobs.

BOOKS

Careers in Retail Sales Management. Research No. 222, Career Research Monographs. Chicago: The Institute for Research, 1996. Detailed information covering all aspects of retail sales management.

Harvey, Christine. *Secrets of the World's Top Sales Performers*. Holbrook, MA: Bob Adams Inc., 1990. Descriptions of the winning techniques of the top salespeople in big companies. The book gives action steps to follow.

Lawhon, John. *Selling Retail*. Tulsa, OK: J. Franklin, 1986. Contains interviews with top retail salespeople and a step-by-step plan for the reader.

Lipow, Valerie. *Retailing Career Starter: Move Ahead in this Fast Growing Field*. New York: Learning Express, 1998. This is a great book to read if you're interested in a career in retailing. It provides all kinds of information about the retail industry, including alternatives to traditional retail careers and industry contact lists to help you get started.

Marcus, Stanley. *Minding the Store*. Boston: Little, Brown, 1974. This book, by the former owner of one of America's best-known retail stores, Neiman Marcus, shows how he succeeded by setting standards for treating customers.

Specter, Robert, and Patrick McCarthy. *The Nordstrom Way*. New York: John Wiley and Sons, 1995. Describes how the Nordstrom family established one of the finest retail stores by offering outstanding customer service.

Underhill, Paco. *Why We Buy: The Science of Shopping*. New York: Simon & Schuster, 1999.
An entertaining look at shopping habits. The author gives concrete and usable advice on how to adapt to the changing customer.

PERIODICALS

Stores
325 7th Street NW, Suite 1100
Washington, DC 20004
(202) 626-8101
Web site: http://www.stores.org
This magazine, published by the National Retailer Federation, has both a print and an online component. Articles and features about retail will interest anyone hoping to work in the industry.

2

PUBLISHER SALES REPRESENTATIVE

If you love to read, you could join the world of publishing by becoming a sales representative for a publishing company. In this job, you will deal with books by persuading bookstores to buy the ones your company publishes.

Publishers sell books to wholesalers, bookstores, schools, libraries, and, occasionally, to individuals. To do this, a publishing house has a sales department. The size of the department varies according to the size of the company. Larger houses have a sales manager who supervises the company's full-time sales representatives. Smaller houses have a sales manager who supervises work commissioned to sales representatives, who are usually part-time.

Sales reps generally have their own territory, and they are responsible for all of the company's customers within that territory. New sales reps usually are given the least lucrative areas. The representative travels to all the places in the territory that sell books. This may include bookstores, discount stores, and grocery stores. He or she carries samples to each store and shows them to the store's book buyer. The samples include books, book jackets, and descriptions of upcoming releases.

A sales representative makes the most of his or her time with the book buyer. Selling best-sellers is an easy job, but getting a buyer to purchase books by lesser-known authors is much harder. The sales representative must know what kinds of books people in the area want to read. Selling a book on advanced physics might not be profitable in some communities.

Publishers' sales representatives attend sales conferences at least twice a year in the spring and fall. At these meetings, the editors present the books that the representatives will be selling. The goal of these conferences is to get the sales representatives excited about the new books. The conference also gives the representatives a chance to talk about which books they think they can sell. Sales representatives try to strike a balance between which books will sell and which books have merit even though they might not sell as well. They are challenged by the fact that they are often persuading buyers to take a chance on a book that has not yet been published.

Sales representatives have an advantage in their selling because publishers allow buyers to return unsold books—called remainders—within a limited amount of time. A buyer can safely order more books than he or she thinks will sell knowing that the only cost for unsold books will be the freight to return them to the publisher. This is great for the buyer and the representative, but tough on the publishing house. Approximately 30 percent of the books that are ordered are returned unsold. Publishers warehouse them for a time and then sell them to remainder dealers.

Publishing houses may have a special division that sells books to schools, universities, and libraries. Since school orders are often large, the representatives work out discount plans with the customers and help them get appropriate

Publisher sales representatives often make presentations at book fairs, where they show off their companies' books.

4000
RELIGIOUS/SPIRITUAL/
INSPIRATIONAL
spirituality.com
CANADA
COMMON SENSE RADIO
OLIVER
NORTH
hugs

books. These school and library consultants talk with librarians, teachers, and professors to find out their needs.

As you advance in this career, you may become a sales manager or a sales director. Both of these titles mean you will be supervising other members of the sales force.

Sales representatives spend long hours on the road and carry heavy bags of samples. The job can be rewarding, however, because books and booksellers are varied and fascinating. There can be quite a bit of travel involved, and the representative may have a chance to read the books he or she sells.

Education and Training

Many sales representatives learn the job by accompanying an experienced representative in the field. An interest in books is more important than an advanced education. Bookstore owners like to think of themselves as a special group whose service appeals to the intellect in others. A successful sales representative will show the same respect for books.

Salary

Sales representatives who work for a large publishing house receive a salary plus expenses. This might be around $30,000 for an entry-level job. Commissioned sales

The Interview

The following are some questions you may be asked in an interview. Thinking about these questions and your answers will not only help you in a job interview but will also give you some insight into yourself.

- What are your long-range career objectives?
- Why did you select this career?
- What are the rewards you expect from your career?
- What qualifications do you bring to the job?
- Why did you choose our company?
- Why should we hire you?
- What have you done that makes you the most satisfied?
- Are you interested in more education and training?

representatives who are independent and work for several companies get a 5 to 10 percent commission and are not reimbursed for expenses.

Outlook

In spite of predictions that television and the Internet will make the printed word obsolete, people are still reading books. Sales of hardback books were down slightly in 2001, but sales of paperbacks went up. Chain bookstores and online bookstores may be changing the way people buy books, but they are not changing people's interest in books.

FOR MORE INFORMATION

ASSOCIATIONS

American Booksellers Association
Web site: http://www.bookweb.org
This site has news from the Association of Independent Bookstores.

Association of American Publishers (AAP)
71 Fifth Avenue
New York, NY 10003-3004
(212) 255-0200
Web site: http://www.publishers.org
The AAP's mission is to expand the market for American books and other published works in all media. Its Web site has a link to employment opportunities.

Association of Canadian Publishers
110 Eglinton Avenue West, Suite 401
Toronto, ON M4R 1A3
Canada
(416) 487-6116
Web site: http://www.publishers.ca

According to its Web site, the Association of Canadian Publishers represents more than 140 Canadian-owned book publishers and encourages the writing, publishing, distribution, and promotion of Canadian books. The site also offers tips for finding a job in publishing.

National Association of Independent Publishers' Representatives
111 East 14th Street
Zeckendorf Towers, Suite 157
New York, NY 10003
(888) 624-7779
Web site: http://www.naipr.org
The National Association of Independent Publishers' Representatives is a support group for publishers' representatives. See its link in the Web Sites section below for information specific to sales and marketing.

WEB SITES

A Career in Publishing
http://www.wiley.com/cda/sec/0,,162,00.html
This Web page, from John Wiley & Sons publishing house, offers job listings and descriptions.

Marketing Advice for the Very Small or Self-Publisher
http://www.naipr.org/marketing.html
This page, part of the National Association of Independent Publishers' Representatives' Web site, takes you through the publishing process. Although the page is geared toward small and self-publishers, the information is still helpful.

BOOKS

Camenson, Blythe. *Opportunities in Publishing Careers*. Chicago: VGM Career Horizons, 1999.
This book is a great overview of the many different career opportunities within the publishing field.

Career as a Bookseller. Research No. 165, Career Research Monographs. Chicago: The Institute for Research, 1998.
This book is written for an audience of bookstore owners, but it does give insight into purchasing practices.

Eaglen, Audrey. *Buying Books: A How-to-Do-It Manual for Librarians*. New York: Neal-Schuman Publishers, Inc., 2000.
The book reviews the entire publishing process, which is essential to understand for anyone who will be working for a publishing house.

Mogel, Leonard. *Careers in Communications and Entertainment*. New York: Simon & Schuster, 2000.
This book gives a perspective of the whole industry, because sales and communications techniques are universal.

PERIODICALS

Publishers Weekly
P.O. Box 16178
North Hollywood, CA 91615-6178
(800) 278-2991
Web site: http://publishersweekly.reviewsnews.com
Publishers Weekly is the bible of the publishing industry. Each issue gives reviews of new books, discusses trends in bookselling, and posts job openings around the country.

3

MANUFACTURER'S SALES REPRESENTATIVE

Have you ever wondered how manufacturers get their products into stores? Maybe someone has come up with a great new stain remover or a wonderful new line of clothing. The product may be great, but no one will know about it unless someone convinces a retail outlet to display and sell the merchandise.

Manufacturers rely on sales representatives to show their merchandise to retail outlets. A manufacturer's sales representative sells the manufacturer's product (cars, groceries, clothing, electronics, and so on) to retail buyers, who then sell the product to the customer. This middle step between manufacturers and consumers is known as the wholesale trade. Manufacturing sales representatives work directly for the manufacturer.

The manufacturer's representative introduces a manufacturer's product to wholesale trade firms, retailers, government agencies, and construction contractors. His or her goal is to get the customer to buy the product. The manufacturer's representative demonstrates the product to show the client how the product is used. He or she describes how it will reduce costs and increase sales, and points out how it differs from similar products. Potential buyers expect the representative to know every detail of the product. Sometimes the sales representative takes a technical expert along to explain the intricacies of the product. Sometimes, it is a challenge just to get a potential buyer to listen. Manufacturer's representatives must be friendly and appealing, and they must be able to work quickly and convincingly.

Once the client has bought the product, the sales rep may offer to help with installation and training the employees in its use. The rep continues to stay in touch with the customer, making sure the product is performing as expected and offering help with displays and promotion. Establishing relationships is very important in this career. Some representatives send their customers letters and cards on anniversaries, birthdays, and holidays. They find that they get and keep more business by treating each customer as if he or she were the most important person on Earth.

In addition to keeping current customers satisfied, the manufacturer's sales representative is constantly recruiting new clients. The representative gets leads from satisfied customers, follows ads in trade magazines, and goes to trade shows and conferences to meet people who are interested in the product. Often the representative entertains prospective clients in the evenings and on weekends, taking them out to dinner, to concerts, and to sporting events.

Manufacturer's representatives usually have sales territories that may cover several states, which means they are on the road for days or weeks at a time. They have to carry heavy bags of samples in and out of buildings. During these trips, they meet with clients during the day and work on presentations or contracts in the evening. In addition, a manufacturer's representative needs to keep ahead of the competition. The representative will spend time learning about new products and keeping track of what others in the field are doing. Representatives have to anticipate what customers will want next year.

Manufacturer's sales representatives must be goal-oriented and persuasive. They need good communication skills. Often they have to work on solving problems. A sales rep must also have patience, since many sales take several months to close. As representatives get more experience, their territories expand and they have more chances to earn larger commissions. Others go into business for themselves once they have learned the basics.

Education and Training

Most employers want to hire sales representatives with proven experience in sales. A person who has taken time to learn about the manufacturer's product stands a better chance of being hired. A new hire generally accompanies an experienced sales rep on the road to learn the ins and outs of the business. Representatives have opportunities to continue their training by attending seminars and taking marketing classes. They can take courses that lead to becoming a certified professional manufacturer's representative.

Salary

Most manufacturer's sales representatives receive a combination of a salary and a commission. Salaries range from $33,000 to upward of $60,000 a year. Representatives for scientific and technical products earn more than those selling groceries and

Visitors at a computer expo test out new computers equipped with flat screen displays. Manufacturer's sales representatives are often involved in exhibiting products at conventions.

clothing. Companies usually pay expenses, such as transportation, hotels, and meals. They may also reward outstanding sales representatives with vacation trips or gifts.

Self-employed manufacturer's agents work for a straight commission, but they have the advantage of being able to set their own schedules.

Outlook

The majority of manufacturer's sales representatives distribute machinery and equipment, groceries, and motor vehicles and parts. Employment is available in almost every part of the country. Manufacturers, especially the smaller ones, will cut costs by using independent agents who are paid only if they sell.

As a whole, job opportunities for sales representatives are expected to grow slowly for the next ten years. Still, customers will continue to need to be shown new products. Sales representatives will become more efficient as computer technology allows them to improve their presentations and to answer customer questions on the spot. Prospective employees should do some research to find out which products are most in demand. Companies selling those products will have the best opportunities.

Industries to Choose From:

Automobiles	Groceries
Beauty supplies	Health products
Chemicals	Housewares
Clothing	Office products
Computers	Plastics
Construction	Sporting goods
Electronics	Telecommunications
Furniture	

FOR MORE INFORMATION

ASSOCIATIONS

Manufacturers' Agents National Association
P.O. Box 3467
Laguna Hills, CA 92654-3467
(949) 859-4040
Web site: http://www.manaonline.org
The group publicizes the role of manufacturers' agents and matches companies and agents.

Manufacturer's Representatives Educational Research Foundation
Box 247
Geneva, IL 60134
(630) 208-1466
Web site: http://www.mrerf.org
This group has certification information.

National Association of Sales Professionals
8300 North Hayden Road, Suite 207
Scottsdale, AZ 85258
(480) 951-4311
Web site: http://www.nasp.com
NASP encourages international participation by those who are interested in obtaining a professional sales certification. Upon acceptance for membership, all candidates are automatically enrolled in the prestigious International Registry of Accredited Salespeople.

WEB SITES

California Occupational Guides
http://www.calmis.cahwnet.gov/file/occguide/MANUSALE.HTM
This is a description of the job of a manufacturer's sales representative, including working conditions, outlook, wages, training requirements, and tips on finding a job.

Career Knowhow
http://www.careerknowhow.com/resumes/samples/salesrep.htm
Gives sample résumés for this position.

Landing a Sales Job with No Experience
http://sales.monsterindia.com/articles/sa_8017
Seven strategies to help you land a job.

Michigan Occupational Information System
http://www.mois.org/scripts/105.HTM
This site provides brief synopses of various careers.

Occupational Outlook Handbook, 2002–03 Edition
http://www.bls.gov/oco
This Web site, published by the U.S. Bureau of Labor Statistics, contains detailed information on hundreds of occupations.

Positive Results Newsletter
http://www.positiveresults.com
This site offers a free monthly newsletter for sales professionals and has in-depth articles, Web site reviews, and inspiring quotes.

Professional Career Development Institute
http://www.pcdi-homestudy.com/index1.html
This group offers home-study courses in fashion merchandising.

Sales Representative in the Retail Industry
http://www.wetfeet.com/asp/RPP_interview.asp?rppid=70&rpName=Roseanne+Zabenoff&type=c
An interview with a manufacturer's sales representative.

Sales Representatives, Technical
http://realvideo.acinet.org/ramgen/49005.rm
Offers a video in RealPlayer format.

Selling Through Manufacturers' Representatives
http://www.era.org/publication/selling.shtml
A brief description of the pros of being a marketing representative.

BOOKS

Career as a Sales Representative Manufacturer's Rep. Research No. 282, Career Research Monographs. Chicago: The Institute for Research, 1998.
This publication outlines everything you need to know about being a manufacturer's sales representative.

Caroselli, Dr. Marlene. *One to One for Sales Professionals*. Madison, WI: CWL Publishing Enterprises, 2001.
This book gives actual scripts to follow when you are giving a sales pitch.

Voss, Jerry. *Soft Sell in a Hard World*. Philadelphia: Running Press, 1998.
The book treats selling as a game and offers practical tips. The reader can jump around to whatever section is the most interesting.

Washburn, Henry. *Why People Don't Buy Things*. Reading, MA: Perseus Books, 1999.
Helps the rep look at the sale from the customer's point of view.

White, Sarah. *Complete Idiot's Guide to Marketing Basics*. New York: Simon & Schuster, 1997.
This book has everything you ever wanted to know about marketing, in a readable style.

4

PRODUCT DEMONSTRATOR

If you like hands-on activities, and if you like the notion of selling things to people, you may want to try working as a product demonstrator. You've probably seen demonstrators at work. At home shows, they demonstrate blenders, jewelry cleaners, and vacuum cleaners. At the grocery store, they offer new kinds of food. Basically, demonstrators show new products to the public, answer their questions, and try to get them to buy.

A demonstrator starts the day by setting up his or her display and making sure the area is clean and will attract customers. As customers come by, the demonstrator shows what the product can do or offers food samples. The demonstrator may also give out coupons, discount tickets, rebate offers, and brochures about the product. Often demonstrators use visual aids, such as charts, survey results, slides, or videos, to promote the product.

The demonstrator must be thoroughly familiar with the product. The goal is to show the customer that the product is easy to use and will be of real use in the kitchen or the house. Food promoters show customers that the food is easy to prepare and that it tastes better than similar foods on the market. Cosmetic demonstrators may give cus-tomers makeovers using the company's products. Demonstrators are expected to give the customers detailed information and to answer questions about the product. Demonstrators try to get the names of prospective buyers so they can follow up with them after the show. Many times this is done by offering a drawing or raffle, which requires the customer to fill out a form with his or her name and phone number.

The demonstrator's job isn't over when the show or the store closes. Demonstrators keep records of the number of coupons and samples given away. They write down approximately how many people they talked with, the questions asked, and details such as the weather (a blizzard would mean fewer customers than a nice spring day). These records help them improve their presentations. Demonstrators clean up their area and take down the display. Food demonstrators may have to bring their own tables, tablecloths, cooking equipment, and utensils.

Demonstrators work in a variety of locations in every part of the country. These might include department stores, grocery stores, shopping malls, convention centers, outdoor fairs, and the backs of trucks. They are on their feet for long periods of time and have to carry heavy loads to set up and dismantle the displays. Demonstrators often work evenings and weekends. Some may travel frequently. Most of the work is part-time and temporary. Demonstrators like the challenge of meeting new people and convincing them to buy a product.

Education and Training

In this field, personal qualities count more than education, although most demonstrators have a high school diploma.

A Coinstar representative shows how one of the company's kiosks counts 600 coins a minute. A demonstrator should test run a product to make sure it works before giving a demonstration.

Employers look for people who are at ease when speaking in public. They want demonstrators who have a sense of humor and who are interested in the products they manufacture. A knowledge of a foreign language could expand the opportunities for demonstrators. Demonstrators work on their own, and they should be able to set up their work and do the required paperwork without supervision.

Employers give demonstrators training in the use of the product. The length of the training varies. Complex products such as computers will take more training time than will learning about a vacuum cleaner. The training may also cover aspects of dealing with customers.

A person who shows a knack for selling as a demonstrator may advance to other marketing jobs, such as manufacturer's representative or other positions in retail sales. If you work for a department store, you might be able to advance into other sales positions within the company.

Salary

Wages vary from minimum wage to as high as $20 per hour. Most demonstrators make between $8 and $13 per hour. This includes the time needed to set up and take down the display.

In some cases, food demonstrators who work in grocery stores must belong to a union. These demonstrators start at

It is important for a product demonstrator to present a pleasant, friendly face to the public. People may lose interest in a product if the demonstrator seems unapproachable.

union wages, which are about $8 per hour. A demonstrator working for a department store might also be eligible for benefits and pension contributions.

Outlook

As trade shows increase in number and size, jobs as demonstrators are expected to grow faster than most other occupations. One of the features of these shows is the demonstrators who can entice customers to stop by and

Finding the Job

- Register with demonstrator–market research firms
- Sign up with a temporary agency
- Apply at department stores
- Ask demonstrators how they got their jobs
- Check newspaper ads
- Register with the state job service

listen to their talk. Customers like the personal touch they get from demonstrators. Studies have shown that sales go up when demonstrators also sell products. Many companies are putting more of their marketing budget into demonstrations.

Employers have trouble finding good people to work in these part-time, short-term positions. Anyone with skills in this area should have no trouble finding work.

FOR MORE INFORMATION

ASSOCIATIONS

American Marketing Association
250 South Wacker Drive, Suite 200
Chicago, IL 60606
(800) 262-1150
Web site: http://www.marketingpower.com
The Web site of the American Marketing Association is a great resource for anyone interested in a job in sales or marketing. Check out the "Careers" section for job postings across the country and other career resources to help you get started.

WEB SITES

California Occupational Guides
http://www.calmis.cahwnet.gov/htmlfile/subject/guide.htm
This is a description of the job of a product demonstrator, including working conditions, outlook, wages, training requirements, and tips on finding a job.

Career Details: Demonstrators and Product Promoters
http://www.xap.com/career/careerdetail/career41-9011.html
This site gives details on the tasks involved in product demonstration.

Demonstrators and Promoters
http://icpac.indiana.edu/careers/career_profiles/100297.xml
A list of job descriptions, wages, and outlook, along with a detailed list of work activities.

The Hill Group
http://www.hillgroup.com
This group gives sales seminars; its Web site offers tips for running a booth at a trade show.

Merchandise Demonstrator
http://www.businesstown.com/businessopps/newbiz-a1000.asp
This Web site offers suggestions for getting started in the business by networking with large companies. It also covers the downside of the job.

Tips for Event Personnel
http://www.allstoredemos.com/tips.htm
Outlines the procedures for demonstrating food products.

Trade Show Advisor
http://www.tradeshowadvisor.com
Provides tips for giving a successful demonstration.

BOOKS

Bayan, Richard. *Words That Sell*. Chicago: Contemporary Books, 1984. This book has 2,500 key words and phrases that make a difference in getting a sale. For example, "In a class by itself," "User-friendly," "Absolutely free," and "You deserve the best."

Brescoll, James. *Opportunities in Sales Careers*. Chicago: VGM Career Books, 2002.
According to a review, "*Opportunities in Sales Careers* offers job seekers essential information about a variety of sales careers and includes training and education requirements, salary statistics, and professional and Internet resources."

Camenson, Blythe, and Jan Goldberg. *Real People Working in Sales and Marketing*. New York: McGraw-Hill, 1996.
The authors of this book offer advice from people who make their living in sales.

Wechsler, Warren. *The Six Steps to Excellence in Selling: The Step-by-Step Guide to Effective Selling*. Edina, MN: Better Books, 1995.
This short book gets down to the essentials of selling.

5

INSURANCE AGENT

If you like to help people and don't mind working on your own, you might want to look into a career as an insurance agent. Insurance agents sell policies that give people protection for their lives, health, and property. When a client has a loss, the agent helps the policyholder settle the claims. Agents get to know their clients and suggest changes in the policies as changes occur in the lives of the clients.

Insurance agents may work either for a company or independently. An agent who works for one company sells only that company's policies. An independent agent can give clients a choice of policies from several companies. Some agents specialize in one kind of insurance. Others sell a variety of policies—life, health, disability, long-term care, property, and casualty insurance.

An insurance agent is constantly seeking new clients. Agents find clients in a variety of ways. They may send out mailings to promote their services. They read the newspaper to learn of new people in the community. They join groups so they can network with others. And they hope that satisfied clients will recommend them to their friends.

Once an agent has a client, the agent meets with the client to discuss the person's insurance needs. If the client is interested in life insurance, the agent must be able to explain the types of life insurance. These include whole life, term, death payments, mortgage payments, college education, and annuities for retirement income. After this first meeting, the insurance agent writes an insurance plan to meet the client's

An insurance agent takes notes as he assesses flood damage to a building. Clients rely on their insurance agents to follow up on their claims and represent their interests.

needs and budget. For health insurance, the agent checks the various offerings to find one that fits the client's family. The sale is closed when the agent and the client have agreed on a policy and the client has filled out an application, taken a physical exam if necessary, and paid the first premium. Some sales are easy, and some take weeks to close.

Agents follow up regularly with their clients to make sure a policy is still covering a client's needs and to see if more insurance is needed. If a client has suffered a property loss, the agent will help him or her get estimates for repairs and get the claim settled as quickly as possible.

Successful agents take a personal interest in their clients' lives. They keep track of moves, promotions, new members of the family, teenage drivers, and college students. They can suggest increased or decreased coverage to their customers as their needs change, and they can let the client know when better coverage is available. These agents are the ones who get repeat business.

Education and Training

High school graduates with proven sales abilities are good candidates for insurance agents. Agents should also have good computer skills. The Internet allows agents to compare policies and prices. Software packages let agents try different policies to find the best fit for the client. The ability to speak another language is an asset for agents who work in communities in which there is a large non-English-speaking population.

Insurance sales agents must get a license in the states where they sell insurance. Licensing involves taking pre-licensing courses and passing a state examination. Most states also require continuing education for agents to keep up with the new rules. Some professional organizations offer programs to certify agents in various specialties. This lets the client know that the agent understands the policy.

Salary

Insurance agents who work for a company are usually compensated through a combination of salary and commission. Most of them earn about $40,000 their first year, in addition to receiving benefits. Agents in a company can work their way into management positions.

Independent agents are paid solely on commission, a percentage of the premiums paid by the clients. They don't receive benefits, but they may receive higher commissions than do salaried workers.

Outlook

This occupation is predicted to grow more slowly than the average occupation. With the Internet, clients can do their

It is important for the insurance agent to explain exactly what is covered under an insurance policy and to help clients select the coverage that is right for them.

own preliminary searches for policies and prices and then go directly to the company.

The demand for various insurance policies is constantly changing, and the agent who can sell a variety of products will have good job prospects. The sale of life insurance is down, but as the population ages there will be a demand for long-term care insurance and annuities. As the population grows, more people will need automobile and home insurance.

Individuals and businesses will always need insurance, regardless of economic conditions.

Types of Life Insurance

Term Least expensive, usable only as a death benefit.

Ordinary life Can be converted to live on during retirement.

Limited payment plan Insured pays the policy off in a certain number of years.

Comprehensive insurance plan Protects a business from loss, such as the death of a partner or employee.

Group plan Selected by a company and paid for by employees through payroll deductions.

FOR MORE INFORMATION

ASSOCIATIONS

The Council of Insurance Agents and Brokers
701 Pennsylvania Avenue NW, #750
Washington, DC 20004-2608
(202) 783-4400
Web site: http://www.ciab.com
The professional association for commercial insurance agents.

Independent Insurance Agents of America
127 South Peyton Street
Alexandria, VA 22314
(800) 221-7917
Web site: http://www.independentagent.com
In addition to providing information to agents, this group has a Young Agents Program.

The National Alliance for Insurance Education and Research
P.O. Box 27027
Austin, TX 778755
(800) 633-2165
Web site: http://www.scic.com
Offers a broad selection of continuing education and professional development programs.

National Association of Insurance Women (International)
P.O. Box 4410
Tulsa, OK 74159
(800) 766-6249
Web site: http://www.naiw.org
The National Association of Insurance Women is a professional organization for women in the insurance industry. The association provides education, networks, and career information to its members.

National Association of Professional Insurance Agents
400 North Washington Street
Alexandria, VA 22314
(703) 836-9340
Web site: http://www.pianet.com
This association has news and information about insurance agents and the insurance industry, and follows federal insurance legislation.

WEB SITES

Canada Career Consortium
http://www.careerccc.org/careerdirections
This site gives good descriptions of jobs and of personality traits for individuals seeking them. Some of the details are specific to Canada.

Insurance News Net
http://www.insurancenewsnet.com
This Web site offers current news and commentary from the insurance world.

Michigan Occupational Information System
http://www.mois.org/scripts/104.HTM
This site provides brief synopses of various careers.

Mutual of Omaha
http://www.mutualofomaha.com/careers
Highlights some job openings and the accompanying duties and qualifications at one of the country's largest insurance companies.

Occupational Outlook Handbook, 2002-03 Edition
http://www.bls.gov/oco
This Web site, published by the U.S. Bureau of Labor Statistics, contains detailed information on hundreds of occupations.

BOOKS

Career as a Life Insurance Agent. Research No. 40, Career Research Monographs. Chicago: The Institute for Research, 1996.
Detailed information covering all aspects of being an insurance agent.

Introduction to Life Underwriting. Dearborn, MI: Dearborn Publishing Company, 1991.
A textbook for a self-study course.

Walsh, James. *What Do You Mean, It's Not Covered?* Santa Monica, CA: The Merritt Company, 1995.
A detailed review of insurance policies and what is and is not covered.

PERIODICALS

American Agent and Broker
330 North Fourth Street
St. Louis, MO 63102
(314) 421-5445
Web site: http://www.agentandbroker.com
American Agent and Broker is a monthly magazine for insurance agents and brokers. Its aim is to help insurance professionals sell more products and services and operate their business more profitably.

Thompson's World Insurance News
62 Frankdale Avenue
Toronto, ON M4J 4A2
Canada
(416) 461-6365
Web site: http://www.thompsonsnews.com
Thompson's World Insurance News is Canada's number one provider of insurance news, offering both a print and online version to insurance professionals.

6

REAL ESTATE AGENT

If you would like to help people make one of the most significant decisions of their lives, a career as a real estate agent might be right for you. Buying a house is a big investment and a complex transaction. Most buyers use a real estate agent to guide them through the process. The real estate agent helps home-buyers with this decision by finding

FOR SALE

HARTFORD REALTY
954-426-5600

and showing properties, arranging financing, and closing the sale.

A real estate agent is an independent worker who contracts with a licensed real estate broker. The broker, who may own a real estate firm, supervises the agents and pays them a portion of the commission from the sale of the property.

Real estate has many specialties. In addition to selling houses, real estate agents sell apartments, office buildings, commercial buildings, industrial buildings, and farmland.

Successful real estate agents work well with people. The agent has to know what the client needs and wants in a space. The agent's goal is not just to sell a house (or an office space or apartment) but to sell a house that will make the buyer happy. The agent also helps buyers make decisions by offering expert advice. This might range from whether a wall can be removed to make a room larger to whether or not to include the existing appliances in the deal.

The agent needs negotiating skills to work out a final price between the buyer and the seller. A real estate agent has to be detail-oriented. Because a real estate sale is a legal transaction, the agent must make sure that the title to the property is clear (has no existing ownership claims on it), the financing is approved, and that the many legal papers are ready at the time of closing.

A job in real estate is not a nine-to-five job. People who are looking for houses are generally at work during the day, so a real estate agent must be available in the evenings and on weekends to show houses. Independent contractors do not get paid vacations or holidays. Some weekends are spent hosting open houses, where prospective buyers can view the property without making an appointment.

In addition to showing houses to buyers, real estate agents must get listings—that is, they must find owners who will let the agent list the property for sale. The listing agent gets a portion of the selling price if another agent actually sells the house. Agents get listings through mailings, going door to door in a neighborhood, holding open houses, and by referrals from satisfied clients. One popular method of getting listings is to send cards with the agent's photo and listings of sports schedules, civic phone numbers, or obscure holidays. The agent hopes that when a person decides to sell a house, he or she will remember that particular agent.

Education and Training

In the United States, real estate agents must be licensed in the state in which they do business. Some states require an agent to take a real estate course (about thirty to ninety classroom hours) before taking the licensing exam. These

A couple and their real estate agent close the deal on a house. Real estate agents represent the interests of both buyers and sellers, and much of their job involves bringing the two together.

courses cover ownership and transfer of real estate, state regulation, mortgages, financing, federal fair housing law, and consumer protection law. Brokers take additional courses that include real property law, contract law, property management, and appraisal.

High school courses in English, math, psychology, and economics will help you prepare for a career in real estate. One of the best ways of training for a successful real estate career is to get to know the community in which you will be working. Learn about the schools, recreation opportunities, and shopping areas. Become familiar with the zoning laws and the homeowners' covenants. The more you know, the more you can target the right house for a buyer.

Salary

Most real estate agents earn about $27,000 per year through commissions, although there is no limit to what a good agent can make. Brokers make about $47,000 per year. The commissions are usually divided among the listing agent and broker, and the selling agent and broker. An agent can expect to receive about half of what the firm gets. An agent who both lists the property and sells it makes the most money.

Outlook

One of the most far-reaching developments in real estate is the use of the Internet to list and show real estate. Now prospective buyers can take a virtual tour of a property without leaving home. Agents must know how to present these properties in the best light in order to entice the buyers to see it in person. As more people use the Internet to check out real estate, agents have more time to secure listings and help close sales.

The real estate profession is moving toward national franchises. Advertising by large, national firms allows the name to become well known. This familiarity draws people to the local branch office of that realty company.

The real estate market has its ups and down, but people will always want to buy and sell houses, commercial property, and land. As long as the demand for real estate exists, real estate professionals will also be in demand.

FOR MORE INFORMATION

ASSOCIATIONS

National Association of Independent Real Estate Brokers
7102 Mardyke Lane
Indianapolis, IN 46226
(317) 547-4679
Web site: http://nationalrealestatebrokers.org
The National Association of Independent Real Estate Brokers is a professional organization that offers training, networking, and public relations to real estate agents and brokers.

National Association of Real Estate Brokers, Inc.
9831 Greenbelt Road
Lanham, MD 20706
Web site: http://www.nareb.com
This association promotes excellence in the real estate industry by encouraging members to share ideas and further educate themselves.

National Association of Realtors
700 11th Street
Washington, DC 20001
Web site: http://www.nar.realtor.com
Another professional association for real estate agents and brokers.

WEB SITES

Michigan Occupational Information System
http://www.mois.org/scripts/106.HTM
This Web site provides short summaries of many careers and describes the general job tasks and work environment.

Occupational Outlook Handbook, 2002–03 Edition
http://www.bls.gov/oco
This Web site, published by the U.S. Bureau of Labor Statistics, contains detailed information on hundreds of occupations.

Real Estate Sales Agent
http://realvideo.acinet.org/ramgen/43008.rm
Offers a video in RealPlayer format.

BOOKS

Evans, Mariwyn. *Opportunities in Real Estate Careers*. Lincolnwood, IL: NTC Publishing Group, 1997.
This book offers essential information about a variety of careers within the real estate industry. It provides additional details about training, salary, and resources.

Floyd, Charles F., and Marcus T. Allen. *Real Estate Principles*. Chicago: Dearborn Financial Pub., 1997.
A textbook used in introductory real estate classes. Gives you some study exercises to try on your own.

Friedman, Jack P., Jack C. Harris, and J. Bruce Lindeman. *Dictionary of Real Estate Terms*. Hauppauge, NY: Barron's Educational Series, 2000.
A listing of every real estate term you could possibly think of.

Irwin, Robert. *Home Buyers' Checklist*. New York: McGraw-Hill, 2002.
By reviewing the questions homebuyers should ask, you'll be able to have the answers for them.

Kennedy, Danielle. *How to List and Sell Real Estate in the 21st Century*. Upper Saddle River, NJ: Prentice Hall, 1999.
Offers sales methods and a twenty-one-day self-training course.

Lee, Michael. *Opening Doors, Selling to Multicultural Clients*. Winchester, VA: Oakhill Press, 1999.
A good book for understanding differences in cultures that affect sales.

Masi, Mary. *Real Estate Career Starter: Finding and Getting a Good Job*. New York: Learning Express, 2001.
Covers most of the field, including education, finding a job, licensing, and success on the job.

Pivar, William. *Real Estate Exam Guide*. Real Estate Education Co., 2000.
Gives examples of potential questions on the real estate licensing exam.

Reis, Ronald A. *The Everything Hot Careers Book*. Holbrook, MA: Adams Media Corp., 2001.
This book gives the inside scoop on real estate careers with interviews with people in the profession.

Shim, Jae K., Joel G. Siegel, and Stephen W. Hartman. *Dictionary of Real Estate*. New York: J. Wiley, 1996.
In addition to real estate terms, the book shows parts of houses, mortgage tables, and measurement tables.

Zeller, Dirk. *Your First Year in Real Estate*. New York: Random House, 2001.
The book gives step-by-step suggestions to challenge you to go from novice to professional.

7

TRAVEL AGENT

If the idea of traveling to exotic places appeals to you, consider becoming a travel agent. Travel agents encourage people to see the world and help them make all the arrangements necessary for a successful trip. Businesses often use travel agents, counting on the agents to find the best deals.

Most travel agents work for a travel agency. Some work for tour companies or hotel chains. A travel agent spends most of the workday behind a desk, talking with customers in person or on the phone, making reservations, and completing paperwork. A computer is essential for helping the agent find the best fares and make reservations. An agent must be accurate and meticulous. People take their travel very seriously, and even one mistake from the travel agent can result in a lost customer.

Customers may come to travel agents with an itinerary already planned. With the agent's extensive knowledge of airlines, trains, hotels, and restaurants, the customer can make decisions about how to go and where to stay on arrival. The agent makes reservations for airline flights, hotels, and car rentals. For travel outside the country, the customer counts on the agent for information about passports, visas, immunizations, and currency exchange rates.

Some customers come to travel agents with only a general idea of what they want to do. Once an agent finds out a customer's interests, time frame, and budget, the agent offers many suggestions. Agents have information on cruises, group tours, special-interest trips (bird watching in Australia, for instance), and destinations. After the customer and the agent plan the trip, the customer can leave with the confidence that the agent will make all the arrangements. All the customer has to do is pack and pick up the tickets.

The travel agent's job isn't always over when clients set off on their trip. They must be prepared to deal with any glitches that may happen along the way.

Many travel agents have ongoing relationships with companies and corporations to do all of their travel arrangements. The agent keeps track of the preferences of each traveler. When an employee of one of the companies calls, all the agent needs is the name, destination, and dates of travel. The agent already knows if the person likes the aisle, middle, or window seat; what time of the day the person likes to travel and on what airline; and what kind of rental car the person prefers. This gives the agent a steady income, and relieves the business from having to take time to make the arrangements.

Travel agents normally work eight-hour days during the week, although during vacation season agents may have to put in overtime. They may also have to be at the office in the evenings or on the weekends for customers to pick up their tickets. Travelers often change their plans, and an agent must be ready to accommodate this. The agent can't necessarily relax once the customer has left on a trip. When tickets get lost, when a rental car isn't there, or when a tour company folds, the agent must try to rescue the vacation for the traveler.

Education and Training

Most travel agents have taken specialized training courses. Vocational schools, adult education programs, and community colleges often offer six- to twelve-week courses for travel agents. The American Society of Travel Agents also offers a correspondence course, and travel agencies provide on-the-job training.

All travel agents need to know how to use computers. Airline, hotel, and car rental reservations are all made by computer. In addition, fluency in another language will allow you to make unique arrangements.

Travel experience is almost essential for an agent. If you have visited another city, region, or country, you will be enthusiastic about persuading others to go to the same

Travel agents need to know how to communicate well. Much of their time is spent on the phone making travel plans with clients and making reservations with other travel and hospitality providers.

place. Resorts and tour companies sometimes send travel agents to a particular destination so the agent will be able to sell the trip to their clients. Summer work in a hotel or resort is good preparation for the travel industry.

Salary

Starting agents earn about $15,000 per year. With more experience, the salary may go up to $30,000, with agency managers making $33,000. Agents who own their own businesses get income from commissions from airlines, hotels, cruises, and tour operators. They may also charge customers a service fee. Agents get many travel benefits, such as reduced airline rates and discounts on hotels, car rentals, cruises, and tours. Company benefits may include paid vacations and holidays, health insurance, and pensions.

Outlook

Jobs for travel agents are expected to grow more slowly than for other occupations. More people are using the Internet to make their own travel arrangements, and airlines have reduced the amount of the commissions that they pay to travel agencies. International and domestic events can also curtail travel.

On the other hand, with rising household incomes, smaller families, and an increase in the retired population, more people will be traveling on vacations. Agents are starting to offer travel packages at a discount. Not everyone is comfortable using a computer, so there will always be those who turn to a travel agent for their travel plans.

Your First Customers

You are a travel agent. A family of four comes to you wanting to go to Disney World for the Fourth of July holiday. They want to save money by sharing a non-smoking room with two beds. See if you can make all the arrangements using the Internet. Just don't put in a credit card number!

1. Find the cheapest flight on the dates they want to travel, but try to make the trip with only one change of planes. How far ahead do they need to reserve?
2. Make hotel reservations. You will need to know how many rooms and what kind of beds, and whether the rooms are smoking or non-smoking.
3. Arrange for a rental car, or find out about public transportation.
4. Get tickets for Disney World.
5. Compare your price with a package tour, which you can find advertised on travel Web sites or in the travel section of your newspaper.

FOR MORE INFORMATION

ASSOCIATIONS

American Society of Travel Agents (ASTA)
1101 King Street, Suite 200
Alexandria, VA 22314
(703) 739-2782
Web site: http://www.astanet.com
The ASTA is the largest association for travel professionals, including agents and travel-related companies.

International Airlines Travel Agent Network (IATAN)
300 Garden City Plaza, Suite 342
Garden City, NY 11530-3302
(516) 663-6000
Web site: http://www.iatan.org
According to its Web site, the IATAN's mission is "to promote professionalism, administer meaningful and impartial business standards, and to provide cost-effective products, services and educational programs that benefit the travel industry."

WEB SITES

California Occupational Guides
http://www.calmis.cahwnet.gov/file/occguide/TRAVLAGT.HTM
This is a description of the job of a travel agent, including descriptions of working conditions, outlook, wages, training requirements, and information on finding a job.

Occupational Outlook Handbook, 2002–03 Edition
http://www.bls.gov/oco

This Web site, published by the U.S. Bureau of Labor Statistics, contains detailed information on hundreds of occupations.

Questions and Ideas About Working in the Travel Industry
http://www.geocities.com/ResearchTriangle/1896/Travelagent.html
Provides information on being a travel agent and links to travel schools.

Travel Agent
http://realvideo.acinet.org/ramgen/43021.rm
Offers a video in RealPlayer format.

BOOKS

Boyd, Wilma. *Travel Agent*. New York: Arco, 1984.
This book has been around for many years, but it is packed with illustrations and relevant information.

Career as a Travel Agent. Research No. 184, Career Research Monographs. Chicago: The Institute for Research, 1997.
Detailed discussion of all aspects of a career as a travel agent.

Reis, Ronald A. *The Everything Hot Careers Book*. Holbrook, MA: Adams Media Corp., 2001.
This book gives the inside scoop on travel agent careers, including interviews with people in the profession.

PERIODICALS

Condé Nast Traveler
4 Times Square
New York, NY 10036
Web site: http://www.concierge.com
This magazine features travel deals and destinations. Its online version offers links to airline, car, and hotel reservations, and offers numerous resources for those planning vacations.

National Geographic Traveler
1145 17th Street NW
Washington, DC 20036
Web site: http://www.nationalgeographic.com/traveler
A travel magazine with feature stories and vivid photography highlighting all kinds of locations around the world.

Travel and Leisure
c/o American Express Publishing
1120 Avenue of the Americas
New York, NY 10036
Web site: http://www.travelandleisure.com
This consumer magazine offers everything a traveler needs to know.

WAITER OR WAITRESS

Many people think that waiting tables is just something to do until the job of their dreams comes along. If you are interested in food, look forward to meeting new people, and like to make them comfortable, you might consider a career in food service. You can work in a diner, swanky restaurant, hotel, or resort. You can become the host or hostess, the dining room manager, or a chef, or you can open your own restaurant.

Waiting jobs are available all over the country, in all sizes of restaurants. If you are just starting out, you might try working at a diner that serves breakfast and lunch. In these establishments, your mistakes will be forgiven as you learn the tricks of the trade. You could then graduate to serving dinners at fancier establishments. They require much more experience and knowledge of food, but the rewards—in the form of tips—are often greater.

Waiters and waitresses greet customers, take their orders, serve the beverages and food, add up the check, and clean the area to make it ready for the next group. Before and after a shift, they may also do side work—like cleaning ketchup and mustard containers, filling salt and pepper shakers, washing sugar jars, sweeping, mopping, and polishing—to get the restaurant ready to open or to close down.

Before a dinner shift, waiters and waitresses may also need to learn from the chef or restaurant manager the specials for the evening. This requires a basic understanding about how food is prepared. The waiter or waitress must also be prepared to make recommendations to customers who may not know what they want. Food service is not a job for the weak: Waiters and waitresses are on their feet most of the time they are working. They carry heavy plates, balance glasses on trays, and serve hot coffee. It is important to have both stamina and strength.

With all this work, waiters and waitresses must put on a pleasant face to the public. Food servers are the people who have direct contact with customers, and they are the ones who take the blame if the food is late or isn't prepared properly. They should have a good memory to avoid mixing up orders, to remember who has regular and who has decaffeinated coffee, and to know what the regulars want before they order. Waiters and waitresses should also know how to add up the bill without using a calculator.

Most of the training is on-the-job. Before they start, waiters and waitresses should memorize the menu and learn the abbreviations that the kitchen uses. With practice and observation, a waiter or waitress can learn to carry three or more plates, or two pots of coffee and a pitcher of water.

Waiters and waitresses may be asked for their opinions on the meals they serve, or about what goes into them. The staff should have tried everything so they can answer the questions. In establishments that have specials, the staff must memorize these dishes on a daily basis. Waiters and waitresses must multitask, as customers often request coffee, a clean spoon, or a glass of juice as a waiter or waitress passes by with an armload of orders. Those who can survive this with a smile on their face will be rewarded.

A good food server knows how to be engaging without crowding the customers' space. The waiter or waitress who achieves this is likely to be tipped handsomely.

Education and Training

There are no educational requirements to be a waiter or a waitress. Some cities may have you take a food-handling test. Larger restaurants may give you a few days of training, or you may "shadow" a more established member of the waitstaff. In smaller diners, you are handed an apron and an order pad and are sent out on your own.

Salary

Most food servers get a small salary, which does not have to be minimum wage but must be at least $2.13 an hour. The rest of the wages come from tips. In a small diner, you will get between $1 and $2 per person for breakfast and lunch. For lunches and dinners, your tips will average from 15 to 20 percent of the check. At fancier restaurants, you will make closer to 20–25 percent of the bill. You may have to share your tips with the cooks and the busing staff. Don't be stingy with this and you will get your orders out quickly and your tables cleaned immediately.

Outlook

Even though people cut back on going out to eat during a recession, they may only switch from going out for dinner to going out for lunch. More affluent families and more people over fifty-five will keep the demand for eating out growing. The turnover in this industry is high, and new opportunities constantly present themselves.

Ways to Increase Your Tips

- Smile.
- Get the beverages out right away.
- Always carry a coffeepot with you at breakfast.
- Keep a constant eye on your tables.
- Smile.
- Don't talk with one group at the expense of others.
- Always carry something with you to and from tables.
- Practice memorizing orders, but don't do it if you are just going to forget.
- Smile.

A waiter's or waitress's approach helps to build loyalty among a restaurant's customers, which is essential to its success.

FOR MORE INFORMATION

ASSOCIATIONS

National Restaurant Association (NRA)
1200 17th Street NW
Washington, DC 20036
(202) 331-5900
Web site: http://www.restaurant.org
The NRA is the leading professional organization for the restaurant industry. The association also has an education foundation.

WEB SITES

Hospitality News
http://www.hospitalitynewsgroup.com
This Web site has archived articles on aspects of the service industry.

Occupational Outlook Handbook, 2002–03 Edition
http://www.bls.gov/oco
This Web site, published by the U.S. Bureau of Labor Statistics, contains detailed information on hundreds of occupations.

On the Rail
http://www.ontherail.com
A resource for restaurant and food service workers, with job lists from deli help to chefs.

So You Wanna.com
http://www.soyouwanna.com/site/syws/waiter/waiter.html
A breezy look at the pros and cons of being a waiter or waitress.

Waiter Digest
http://www.schonwalder.org
A site with information on food and wine, as well as some
waiter/waitress humor.

Waiters and Waitresses
http://realvideo.acinet.org/ramgen/65008.rm
Offers a video in RealPlayer format.

BOOKS

Cannon, Howard. *The Complete Idiot's Guide to Starting Your Own Restaurant.* New York: Alpha Books, 2002.
This book includes a chapter on what owners are looking for in employees.

Casado, Matt A. *Food and Beverage Service Manual.* New York: John Wiley and Sons, 1994.
This is a great reference guide for anyone who needs help keeping the big picture of serving patrons in focus. Includes many informative drawings and diagrams.

Dahmer, Sondra, and Kurt W. Kahl. *Restaurant Service Basics.* New York: John Wiley and Sons, Inc., 2002.
A basic manual for servers. In addition to the basics, the book describes service in all types of dining establishments, using computers on the job, and dealing with emergency situations.

Devoss, Lishka. *How to Be a Professional Waiter (Or Waitress): Everything You Need to Know to Get the Right Job, Make Good Money, and Stay Sane.* New York: St. Martin's Press, 1995.
A comprehensive guide with no-nonsense, practical advice on how to make a living as a waiter or a waitress.

Kirkham, Mike, Bill Crawford, and Peggy Weiss. *The Waiting Game: The Ultimate Guide to Waiting Tables.* Austin, TX: Twenty Per Cent LLC, 2000.
As the authors of this book say, "Before you can win you have to know how to play the game," and they do a good job of giving

readers as much information as possible in an entertaining and attention-holding format. This book is even endorsed by First Lady Laura Bush.

Lewis, Leslie. *How to Make Megabucks Waiting Tables*. New York: Bookmark Publishing Corp, 1997.
Lots of tricks of the trade that might take years to learn on your own.

ADVERTISING SALES REPRESENTATIVE

If you are creative, persuasive, and energetic, advertising sales might be the job for you. Advertising sales representatives sell advertising for media outlets, including radio and TV stations and newspapers. Small media companies are good places to start in this career.

An advertising sales representative contacts local businesses and persuades them that their sales will increase if they buy time on the radio or television, or if they take out an ad in the newspaper. Before going out on a sales call, the representative learns about the business. The rep finds out what the business sells—big ticket items such as cars, a variety of goods such as gifts, or a specialty market such as clothing. The rep also finds out who the customers are—working families, seniors, or teenagers. With this knowledge, the rep can target the client. For instance, a store that sells clothing for teens might not want to advertise on a classical music station, and a retirement home would probably not advertise on a rock station.

The representative shows the business owner how advertising in the local media will increase business. When the client decides to buy advertising time or space, the sales representative helps the client choose the format, the length of the ad, and the time slot. After the advertisement has been aired or published, the rep follows up to see if the customer is happy with the ad and suggests changes for future ads.

Advertising sales representatives regularly visit current clients. They check to see if a client wants to buy more time or space. The advertising sales representative tells customers about upcoming promotions and gives them information on discounts and package rates.

Advertising sales representatives love to sell. They are aggressive about going out to drum up business rather than waiting for the customers to come to them. To do this, they make cold calls to businesses that have not yet bought advertising in that media outlet, follow up on referrals from other customers, and send information to potential advertisers. Once a sale is made, the representative must keep track of the ads sold, when and where they appeared or aired, and the agreed-on rates and discounts.

Advertising sales representatives usually work independently and set their own hours. A person who wants to succeed in this field must be organized and have self-discipline. An advertising sales representative is a good listener and knows how to communicate.

Good advertising sales representatives can move up to supervisory positions. Some become independent agents and contract with several media outlets.

Education and Training

Employers in smaller media markets look for people who are creative and show persistence in making a sale. There is a

> Advertising sales representatives make sure that advertisements are correct before they go into a newspaper or on the air. Running ads that are incorrect is a sure way to lose a client.

high turnover in these small markets, so they are good places to start a career. Living in the community for a time is an advantage since you will be familiar with the local businesses and with the makeup of the media audience.

Some employers have training programs for new employees. In other places, the best training comes from going out on the job with an experienced salesperson.

Salary

Entry-level advertising sales representatives start at about $10 per hour. Salaries vary greatly according to the position and location—a representative in New York City will make more than one in Sheridan, Wyoming. Some representatives work on commission. They get from 10 percent to 20 percent of every sale they make.

Advertising sales representatives have no upper limit on the amount they can earn. Simply put, those who sell more earn more.

Outlook

Advertising sales are the lifeblood of the media. Except for public stations that have pledge drives, radio and TV stations depend on advertising to pay their expenses. Newspapers can offer the issues at low prices because of advertising, and free papers depend entirely on advertising for their income. The person who can sell air time and news-paper space will always be in demand.

The field of advertising sales will probably grow faster than the average for the next ten years. Many representatives will expand their client base by selling banner ads and Web advertising on the Internet.

Making the Advertising Work

Good newspaper ads need to stand out. A white-on-black format catches the eye. Use a different font than that of the news text, but don't use too many different fonts in one ad. If a business has a logo, use that in the ad so readers will connect with the business. The ad should have one message, and it should explain how the product or service will benefit the customer.

Radio ads must get the listener's attention within three seconds. They can use the voices of local broad-casters or amateurs, which gives the ad a sincere touch. Radio is all sound, so you can use music and sound effects.

Television ads should not confuse the viewer by showing too much. To get a head start, watch TV ads and figure out what you like and don't like about them.

FOR MORE
INFORMATION

WEB SITES

Advertising Agents and Sales Workers

http://www.adeca.state.al.us/soicc/soicc/WebSTAR3.0/SOICC/socc/3.html

This site describes the duties, education, and salary for these jobs.

Canada Career Consortium

http://www.careerccc.org/careerdir

This site gives good descriptions of jobs and of personality traits for the individuals seeking them.

Marketing Jobs.com

http://www.marketingjobs.com

This site features a search engine to help you wade through the hundreds of jobs available around the country.

Occupational Outlook Handbook, 2002–03 Edition

http://www.bls.gov/oco

This Web site, published by the U.S. Bureau of Labor Statistics, contains detailed information on hundreds of occupations.

BOOKS

Career Opportunities in Advertising and Public Relations. New York: Facts on File, 1996.
This book details the many opportunities in advertising and public relations, with suggestions on how to begin your career.

Dahl, Gary. *Advertising for Dummies*. New York: Hungry Minds, 2001. Although this book is written from the businessperson's point of view, it will help you target your pitch and anticipate questions.

Dennison, Dell. *The Advertising Handbook for Small Business*. Vancouver, BC: Self-Counsel Press, 1994.
Gives suggestions to small businesses to help them make the most of their advertising.

Eastman, Susan Tyler, Douglas A. Ferguson, and Robert A. Klein, eds. *Promotion and Marketing for Broadcasting and Cable*. Boston: Focal Press, 1999.
The book, which explains what media outlets need to make their stations successful, can help sales representatives target a customer's advertising.

Field, Shelly. *Career Opportunities in Advertising and Public Relations*. New York: Facts on File, 1996.
Gives good summaries of many careers in advertising.

Lewis, Herschel Gordon. *On the Art of Writing Copy*. New York: Amacom, 2000.
This book explains the general rules for copywriting and offers examples.

Mogel, Leonard. *Careers in Communications and Entertainment*. New York: Simon & Schuster, 2000.
This book gives a perspective of the entire advertising industry.

Reis, Ronald A. *The Everything Hot Careers Book*. Holbrook, MA: Adams Media Corp., 2001.
This book gives the inside scoop on advertising sales careers, including interviews with people in the profession.

10

FUND-RAISER
FOR NONPROFIT
ORGANIZATIONS

If you are interested in a good cause, or if you belong to a social change organization, you know that you are constantly being asked for money to help support the cause. Why not turn your desire to help the greater good into a career?

Fund-raisers, or development officers, raise money for nonprofit organizations, the tax-exempt groups that strive to make lives better. Fund-raisers talk to potential contributors about the cause for which they are working and convince the contributors that their money will make a difference in the world. Fund-raisers may also plan events such as benefits for the cause, organize direct mailings that inform the public and solicit funds, and enlist volunteers to help with all kinds of work. They keep track of their expenses and the money that is raised. Public speaking may also be part of the job.

Fund-raisers must be very careful to account for the money they raise. Many organizations have lost the support of the public because they used the money in ways the contributors did not intend. Donors also want to know how their money is being used. The fund-raiser needs to keep the contributors up to date on the use of the funds.

One of the biggest jobs of a fund-raiser is to make a database of potential major contributors. This database would contain names, business affiliations, and contact numbers. The fund-raiser does some research to find out which causes the potential donor supports and what organizations that person belongs to. The fund-raiser makes a plan for asking for funds. This might be a meeting in the donor's office, a dinner invitation, or accompanying the fund-raiser to a special event. The fund-raiser prepares written material for the donor to look over. This material explains why the money is needed, what it would be used

Staging a fund-raising event such as the California Aids Ride includes a near round-the-clock effort of attracting and organizing volunteers and soliciting sponsorships and press coverage.

for, and how the donor would be recognized. At this point, the fund-raiser needs to be patient. Big contributions are not made on the spur of the moment.

Many people shy away from fund-raising because they don't like to ask people for money. Unless organizations have money, the good work they are doing will not be able to continue. As a fund-raiser, you have a chance to talk with other people about a cause you believe in and convince them to help you in continuing that good work.

Some of the most important personal characteristics that a fund-raiser needs are a commitment to public service, enthusiasm, idealism, and an ability to deal with people. A fund-raiser is fluent, pays attention to detail, is able to multi-task, knows how to negotiate, and is creative. Fund-raisers must have a good personal appearance when soliciting money. The CEO of a Fortune 500 company will expect the fund-raiser to dress appropriately for the company's office. Because fund-raisers work for organizations they believe in, their satisfaction with their jobs is very high.

Education and Training

There is no formal training for fund-raising, but the job is fairly simple (although it involves hard work) and can be learned easily. Personal qualities are more important in this field than is education. One of the best ways to learn fund-raising is to volunteer for the organization and learn the techniques of the current development director. Find a mentor who will steer you through the work. As you continue, you can attend fund-raising seminars and take classes in nonprofit management. The National Society of Fundraising Executives offers continuing education and certification. In general, you should be as well informed as you can be (try reading the newspaper every day) and should be comfortable with people, especially speaking to groups of them.

Salary

At the outset, if making money is your career goal, do not go into the nonprofit field. Fund-raisers for nonprofits can make anywhere from $10,000 to $150,000 per year, although most of them will be on the lower end of the salary scale. The size of the organization and the geographic region make a difference. Large groups on the coasts pay the most.

Outlook

The sector will continue to grow and will become more competitive as more groups go after the same dollars. Fund-raising jobs will continue to be available because good fund-raisers are hard to find.

Fund-raising Techniques

Direct mail Sending written material to potential contributors.

Special events Organizing races, auctions, or carnivals.

Prospect research Finding out about potential donors and keeping track of this information.

Major donor solicitation Working with people or foundations that can make large contributions.

Planned giving Learning about annuities and wills and encouraging people to donate in this way.

Data records and management Keeping track of information from potential donors for contributions received and acknowledged.

FOR MORE INFORMATION

ASSOCIATIONS

Association of Fundraising Professionals (AFP)
1101 King Street, Suite 700
Alexandria, VA 22314

(703) 684-0410
Web site: http://www.nsfre.org
The AFP is the professional organization for fund-raisers. The association's Web site is full of valuable resources, including a job bank.

WEB SITES

Action Without Borders
http://www.idealist.org
This Web site has job listings, internship and volunteer opportunities, a worldwide Internet community, a newsletter, and a special section for teens.

The Center on Philanthropy at Indiana University
http://www.philanthropy.iupui.edu
This site has information on the importance of philanthropy and the results of studies on the giving habits of Americans.

Fund-raising Forum
http://www.raise-funds.com/698forum.html
Includes suggestions for getting started as a fund-raiser.

Nonprofit Careers & Job Search Information
http://www.yale.edu/career/nfp/salary.html
A comparison of salaries at various nonprofit organizations.

BOOKS

Career as a Professional Fundraiser. Research No. 316, Career Research Monographs. Chicago: The Institute for Research, 1996. Learn more details about the job of fund-raiser, including how to get started in the career, what you can do now to prepare, and what kinds of things you can expect to do on the job.

Dove, Kent E. *Conducting a Successful Capital Campaign*. San Francisco: Jossey-Bass Publications, 2000.
A guide to planning, managing, and running a campaign.

Fischer, Marilyn. *Ethical Decision Making in Fund-Raising*. New York: John Wiley and Sons, 2000.
Helps the fund-raiser make decisions on solicitations in ethically troubling situations.

Flanagan, Joan. *Successful Fundraising*. Chicago: Contemporary Books, 2000.
Gives information on gaining access to funds, building relationships with donors, and raising more money in less time. Offers real-life examples.

Holland, James. *The Concert Book*. Chicago: Bonus Books Inc., 1999.
Follows the planning and successful execution of a major benefit concert.

Reis, Ronald A. *The Everything Hot Careers Book*. Holbrook, MA: Adams Media Corp., 2001.
This book gives the inside scoop on fund-raising careers, including interviews with people in the profession.

Wagner, Lilya. *Careers in Fundraising*. New York: John Wiley and Sons, Inc., 2002.
Everything you wanted to know about becoming a fund-raiser.

Warwick, Mal. *How to Write Successful Fundraising Letters*. San Francisco: Jossey-Bass Publications, 2001.
This book gives examples of successful fund-raising letters, something every development officer needs to know.

Weinstein, Stanley. *Complete Guide to Fund-raising Management*. New York: John Wiley and Sons, 1999.
A practical how-to book that addresses day-to-day problems in fund-raising. The book comes with a computer diskette.

11

LOBBYIST

If you think you would like to change the way things work and you like the high-energy world of politics, you might consider a job as a lobbyist. Lobbying is the right of any person or group to provide information to legislators in order to influence the passage or defeat of legislation. Anyone can lobby. It is a right protected by the First

Amendment of the Constitution. Professional lobbyists make lobbying a full-time job.

Many groups and companies are interested in the legislation that gets passed by state legislatures and by Congress. These groups want to inform the elected officials about their issues and try to convince them to pass bills that will help the group or the company. To do this, companies and groups hire lobbyists.

A lobbyist is a person who is familiar with the interests of the client and with the legislative process. A lobbyist goes to an elected official before a particular law comes up for a vote and discusses with the senator or representative why the company or group wants the bill passed. The lobbyist must try to answer all the questions that the elected official has. Most elected officials are very busy and cannot give a lobbyist more than a few minutes. A lobbyist has to deliver the message in the shortest amount of time.

Lobbyists have to know something about psychology in order to deal with people whose views differ from the lobbyist's point of view. Often lobbyists will be involved in emotional discussions. A good lobbyist listens to the other points of view and doesn't get angry. A lobbyist knows when to

A lobbyist testifies in support of a measure that would change South Dakota's school funding formula in favor of smaller schools. Preparation and persuasion are useful tools in effective lobbying.

compromise, or give up something in order to get something. Lobbyists must know how to communicate both orally and in writing. To be effective, a lobbyist must build a network of contacts. These contacts may include elected officials, government employees, and university professors. A lobbyist can go to these contacts for information or help.

Most lobbyists specialize in one area, such as taxes, transportation, health issues, or the environment. Specializing allows a lobbyist to become an expert in one particular field. Legislators don't have time to become experts on all of the bills that they have to consider. They turn to lobbyists to inform them about issues and to answer their questions.

The majority of a lobbyist's time is not spent talking with legislators, but in doing research, analyzing legislation, following bills through the process, attending hearings, and working with others interested in the same issues.

In the past, lobbyists had no rules governing their conduct. They could take legislators out to a sports event, treat them to an elaborate dinner, and give them gifts. Many times this would "buy" an elected official's vote. This sort of extravagant entertaining gave lobbyists a bad reputation. Laws reforming lobbying practices made these activities illegal. Lobbyists can no longer offer anything that might be considered buying a vote. In addition, state lobbyists must register with their secretary of state, and congressional lobbyists must register with Congress. Lobbyists file quarterly reports showing any expenditures over $500.

Lobbyists should always be prepared to discuss the details of the causes they represent—both to the politicians whose votes they seek and to the general public, whose support is likely to influence the politicians as well.

Lobbyists work long hours, especially when the legislators are in session. They also have to find time to research their areas of interest. Sometimes a lobbyist will spend several years working on one issue. Despite the hard work, many lobbyists find their jobs rewarding and like being able to make a difference in people's lives.

Education and Training

Lobbyists do not have to have any special education. They don't have to pass exams or be licensed. Many of them get their training by working for a state legislator or a congressperson, either as a volunteer or in a paid position. This kind of on-the-job training is one of the best ways for a future lobbyist to learn about the political process.

Since a lobbyist has to communicate a point of view, those with good communications skills will be in demand. Courses in English, communication, and journalism can help you improve your chances of being an effective lobbyist.

Salary

Salaries for lobbyists vary greatly. Those working for large lobbying firms that have many clients can make $50,000 or more per year. Those working for small nonprofit groups make considerably less.

Outlook

As long as this country has elected legislatures, lobbyists will be needed. A person who can learn about a client's business and can convey the client's concerns to legislators will be sought after.

Many states have term limits, meaning that elected officials can serve only a certain number of years. Lobbyists have become more necessary in these states. Term-limited representatives need to learn quickly about the issues they will be debating. Often they turn to lobbyists to give them the needed background information.

Where Did the Term "Lobby" Come From?

One account says that in the early 1800s people waited in the lobby of the New York State Capitol in order to talk to their legislators. Another story says that the lobby of the Willard Hotel was the meeting place for legislators and those who wanted favors done.

FOR MORE INFORMATION

ASSOCIATIONS

American League of Lobbyists (ALL)
P.O. Box 30005
Alexandria, VA 22310
(703) 960-3011
Web site: http://www.alldc.org
This organization represents the interests of lobbyists and encourages ethical lobbying practices. The organization's Web site is full of helpful information, including career resources, event listings, a job bank, and the latest news.

WEB SITES

American Academy of Physician Assistants
http://www.aapa.org/gandp/dos-donts.html
Don't be fooled by the Web site, which is geared toward physician assistants. This page features lists of dos and don'ts for all lobbyists.

Careers in Lobbying
http://careers.cua.edu/handouts/lobbyingcareers.htm
This is a page on Catholic University's career services Web site. Although intended for CU students and alumni, the information will be helpful to all those interested in becoming a lobbyist. The page includes a description of a day in the life of a lobbyist and links to related organizations.

Council of Landscape Architectural Registration Board
http://www.clarb.org/licensure/lobbying.pdf
This page is written for members of the CLA who lobby, but it is a good general guide for anyone wanting to pursue a career in lobbying.

Healthy Sale
http://www.getthatgig.com/nonprofit_political/careers/c_lobbyist_bayer.html
This site features an enlightening interview with a lobbyist.

Lobbying
http://www.cftech.com/BrainBank/GOVERNMENT/Lbby.html
Provides rules for lobbyists in Washington and a list of publications.

Lobbying as a Career
http://www.alldc.org/career.htm
Part of the American League of Lobbyists Web site, this page offers a concise description of lobbying and how to get started in the career.

BOOKS

Reis, Ronald A. *The Everything Hot Careers Book*. Holbrook, MA: Adams Media Corp., 2001.

This book gives the inside scoop on lobbyist careers, including interviews with people in the profession.

Wolpe, Bruce C. *Lobbying Congress: How the System Works*. Washington, DC: Congressional Quarterly Publishing, 1990.
If you're going to become a lobbyist, it is important to understand the government system. Though over a decade old, this book does a good job of covering standards like the rules of lobbying, the lawmaking process, and making contacts.

Zorach, John. *The Lobbying Handbook*. Washington, DC: Professional Lobbying and Consulting Center, 1990.
This 1,000-page book covers it all—the legislative process, contacts, rules for lobbyists, and case studies. Everything you'll need to start your career as a lobbyist.

PUBLICATIONS

Lobbyists, Brief #608
Chronicle Guidance Publications
(800) 622-7284
Web site: http://www.chronicleguidance.com
This brief provides an in-depth look at lobbying as a career choice.

INTERNSHIPS

Washington Intern Foundation
(703) 979-5534
You can learn a lot from working as a government apprentice for a summer, even if you're just making copies and answering phones. Call the Washington Intern Foundation for more information.

12

AUCTIONEER

If you like to talk fast, you could have a lot of fun as an auctioneer. Auctioneers sell almost any-thing—livestock, machinery, cars, furniture, and fine art.

People sell items through an auction because they think they will get more money for their wares. Auctions also have the advan-tage of attracting more potential

There is an element of entertainment to the auctioneer's call. The rhythmic pattern of the auctioneer's voice as he or she solicits bids helps to build excitement for the items being auctioned.

customers for an item than a retail store would. A farmer looking for an antique piece of farming equipment could waste weeks of his or her time searching for it. But the farmer would drive for miles if he'd seen a listing for an auction advertising that piece of equipment.

The auctioneer advertises the sale in order to attract a large crowd. The advertisement should include the date, time, place, type of items to be auctioned, and a description of some of the more popular or unique items. These ads will then be placed in newspapers and on radio and TV stations.

The more the auctioneer knows about the merchandise and the customers, the more effective the advertising will be.

To have a successful auction, the auctioneer must be familiar with the items that are offered for sale. The auctioneer (or the seller) writes out a description for each item. In some cases, a minimum bid is suggested. The auctioneer arranges the goods so that potential buyers can peruse them before the auction. Auction items are arranged in "lots" of similar items—books, furniture, jewelry, and so on.

As the auction starts, the auctioneer's job is to get the buyers excited and in the mood to bid. This is where the auctioneer's bid-calling talent comes in. Bid-calling is the sing-song, almost incomprehensible chant that the auctioneer calls out as bids are taken. Good auctioneers are showy and make jokes during the bidding to keep the audience interested. By getting the buyers to increase their bids, the auctioneer gets a good deal for the seller. Once a sale is made, the auctioneer or an assistant records the sale, gets the purchaser's name and address, collects the money, and arranges for the delivery of the item if necessary.

Agricultural auctioneers work outdoors in all weather conditions. Others may work inside, but they are on their feet for long periods of time. When auctioneers are not conducting an auction, they are checking the market to purchase items to auction and to keep up with current prices.

Auctioneers need a strong voice and the physical stamina to keep the audience energized throughout the auction. Auctions can be stressful, especially when two or more people have their hearts set on the same item. The auctioneer has to have crowd-handling skills to keep people under control and to keep the loser from being too disappointed. The auctioneer's goal is to get people to buy something on the spur of the moment. Many buyers have given in to an auctioneer's routine and have gone away with something that they swore they would never buy. A good auctioneer convinces the buyers that they need the item, establishes the price, and closes the deal. Unlike many other sales, this one happens in a matter of minutes.

A highlight of the auctioneer's year is participation in state-fair bid-calling contests. Auctioneers vie with each other to impress the judges and the audience. The prizes are modest, but the attention is great.

Education and Training

Auctioneers don't need college degrees, but they do need to attend a training school. At this school, they will learn bid-calling, marketing, and advertising, and will get a chance to conduct an auction. These courses last for a few weeks or for a semester. After graduating from the training school, many auctioneers become apprentices, where they help in running an auction business.

Some states require that auctioneers be licensed. The requirements may be met by attending a training school or by working as an apprentice. The candidates for licensing may also be screened to determine if they are of good moral character.

Salary

As with many occupations, the amount you can earn as an auctioneer depends on how much training you have and how much determination you have to succeed. Auctioneers can earn anywhere from $16,000 to $70,000 per year.

Outlook

The popularity of auctions is increasing, as is the need for good auctioneers. Auctioneers are not as affected by a recession as some occupations. Sadly, a recession may mean more auctions, since many people are forced to sell their goods to get quick cash. In addition, auctions are often held to sell the contents of the houses and estates of deceased individuals, which means there will always be a need for auctioneers.

An auctioneer directs the bidding for a sale of Bordeaux wines at Christie's, the London auction house. Christie's is one of the most upscale auction houses in the world.

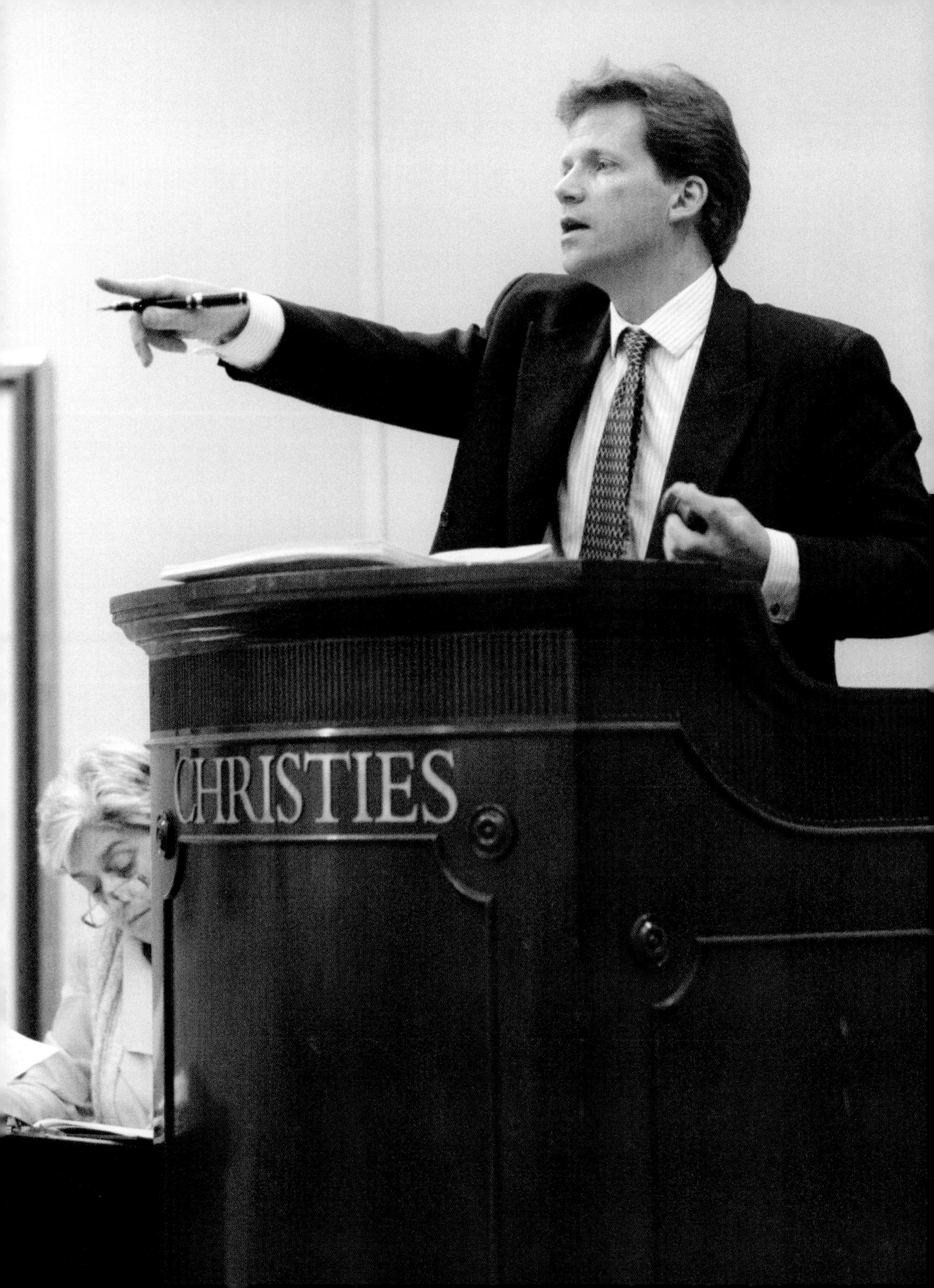
CHRISTIES

A Short List of Auction Terms

Absentee bidder A person who is not at the sale but who submits a top-price bid in advance.

Absolute auction An auction where goods are sold to the highest bidder with no limiting conditions.

Appraisal The process of estimating the value of an item.

As is Selling the item without any sort of warranty.

Bidder number The number issued to each person registered at an auction.

Estate sale The sale of property left by a person who has died.

Reserve bids The minimum price that a seller will accept for an item. If this price is not reached, the auctioneer can pass on the sale.

Tie bids When two or more bidders bid the same price at the same time and the auctioneer has to settle the conflict.

FOR MORE INFORMATION

ASSOCIATIONS

National Auctioneers Association
8880 Ballentine
Overland Park, KS 66214
(913) 541-8084
Web site: http://www.auctioneers.org
The National Auctioneers Association promotes the auction method of marketing and enhances the professionalism of its practitioners. The site has links to auction schools.

WEB SITES

Auctioneer
http://www.careerccc.org/careerdirections/eng/e_oc_dwn.asp?ID=135&Alpha+no
This site gives good descriptions of jobs and of personality traits for the individuals seeking them. Some of the details are specific to Canada.

Auctioneers Training Center
http://www.auctioneerstraining.com
This site has live videos of auctioneer students in training.

Larry Finley Auctioneers and Appraisers
http://www.netwurx.net/~finley/sample2.htm
This site provides a sample of bid-calling.

BOOKS

Haubenstock, Susan, and David Joselit. *Career Opportunities in Art.* New York: Facts on File, 2000.
One of the chapters in this book features a description of jobs in an art auction house.

Herrmann, Frank. *Sotheby's: Portrait of an Auction House.* New York: WW Norton & Company, 1981.
Sotheby's is the world's foremost art auction house. This book reveals the inner workings of the company and talks about the world of collecting.

Reis, Ronald A. *The Everything Hot Careers Book.* Holbrook, MA: Adams Media Corp., 2001.
This book gives the inside scoop on auctioneer careers, including interviews with people in the profession.

PERIODICALS

Antiques and Collecting
1006 S. Michigan Avenue
Chicago, IL 60605
This magazine has articles on what people are collecting and a section on what has sold recently at auction.

SCHOOLS

Auctioneering Training Center
P.O. Box 1461
Regina, SK S4P 3C2
Canada
(888) 999-4555
(306) 757-4271 (outside Canada)

Canadian Auction College
Georgian College of Applied Arts & Technology
92 College Crescent
Barrie, ON L4M 5C8
Canada
(705) 726-2120

Continental Auctioneers School
P.O. Box 346
Mankato, MN 56002-0346
(507) 625-5595

Florida Auctioneer Academy
10376 E. Colonial Drive, Suite 110
Orlando, FL 32817
(800) 422-9155

Harrisburg Area Community College
One HACC Drive
Harrisburg, PA 17110
(717) 780-2300

Oklahoma Auction Real Estate Academy
11220 Dover Court
Yukon, OK 73099
(405) 373-4008

Reading Area Community College
10 South 2nd Street
Reading, PA 19602
(610) 372-4721

Reppert School of Auctioneering
P.O. Box 6
Auburn, IN 46706
(219) 927-9999

Southwestern Ontario School of Auctioneering
RR #5
Woodstock, ON N4S 7V9
Canada
(519) 537-2115

Texas Auction Academy
7075 Elm Street
Frisco, TX 75034
(972) 712-4330

Walton School of Auctioneering
3860 Paradise Road
Medina, OH 44256
(330) 725-8958

Western Canadian School of Auctioneering
64 Berkley Place NW
Calgary, AL T3K 1A7
Canada
(888) 466-6561

Western College of Auctioneering
3918 Highway 312
Billings, MT 59105
(406) 252-7066

World Wide College of Auctioneering
P.O. Box 949
Mason City, IA 50402-0949
(800) 423-5242

13

ART DEALER

If you spend your free hours at the art museum instead of the mall, if you notice the little details in the scenes around you, if a color isn't just red but cerise or cranberry, you might look into a career as an art dealer. Art dealers own or just work at art galleries, the places where the public gets to see and buy the works of up-and-coming

Popular art dealer Philip Mould holds an empty picture frame as he stands in his London gallery. Mould has a reputation for recovering obscure but valuable artwork.

artists. They must be able to function in two very different worlds. One is the artistic world, where the dealer must know a lot about art. The other is the business world, where attention to finance, marketing, and communication takes precedence.

Art dealers must keep up with trends. They have to anticipate what the public wants to buy and which artists are going to be in demand. Most dealers specialize in one area of art—contemporary, expressionism, or pop art, for example. Dealers in successful galleries have a clientele to whom they sell artistic works. A dealer with a lot of contacts will be able to sell almost everything that comes into the gallery. Dealers must spend time cultivating these customers, meeting them at parties, auctions, and gallery openings.

Artists approach dealers by meeting them in person or sending the dealer slides of their work. Most dealers want to work with established artists, so they look for artists who have been in shows or exhibits and have had good reviews, or who have a good track record of selling.

Once the art dealer decides to buy, the art must be priced. The artist holds in his or her hand a work that took years of practicing the craft and many hours to produce. The piece may also have emotional significance. The art dealer looks at the piece and thinks about its potential customers. The dealer has to know if the piece represents a trend that is on the rise or one that is falling out of favor. The dealer adds in the cost of running the gallery and the "rent" for the space until the piece is sold. Then the dealer figures in the reputation of the artist.

The dealer and the artist sign a contract, which includes such terms as the amount of the commission, the length of time the art will be displayed, whether the artist can display work in other galleries, what kind of advertising will be done, and at what point the artist will be compensated.

Art galleries are the places where artists meet their prospective buyers. Galleries hold shows, either of a single

Art dealers show art to clients, get art from artists, and run galleries. Many of them do it because they love to be surrounded by art.

artist or a group of artists. The public is invited to these showings, and refreshments are usually provided. The artists mingle with the public to talk about their work. This personal touch often leads to sales or commissions.

The art dealer has to run the gallery in a businesslike way. The dealer makes sure that everything is displayed in an attractive manner. Walls may have to be moved and lighting changed with each new display. The dealer hangs art so the pieces complement each other. In addition, the dealer has to handle the paperwork for the artist and for the customer. Computers are necessary for keeping track of the client base.

Art galleries are found all over the country, but the most successful ones are often in big cities, where most of the potential buyers live. Many dealers get their start by working in small galleries, where they learn the rules of the business. With a little training, they are ready to work in big city galleries. Galleries have reputations. Some are known to be better places to display certain types of artwork than others. A dealer will take time to do some investigation in order to become associated with a good gallery.

Education and Training

There are no formal educational requirements to be an art dealer. Many people work their way into this field by starting at the bottom. Your first job in an art gallery may be framing, packaging art to ship, or building display tables. Whatever it is, pay attention as you work and learn all you can about the gallery and about art.

Salary

Salaries in art galleries start at about $25,000 per year, and there may be benefits included. With experience, you may be eligible for a commission. Art dealers and gallery owners work on commission, usually 50 percent of the price of a piece of art. An expensive piece of art will bring in a larger commission, but it will also take more time to sell than will several less costly pieces. Many gallery owners do well, but it is probably not a job in which you will make millions. The people who go into this business do it for the love of art and the excitement of being in the art world.

Outlook

Art has been around for as long as civilization, but art galleries are subject to the state of the overall economy. When times are tough, art is one of the first things that consumers cut out of their budgets.

Some artists are starting to show their work on the Internet, but it's not likely that this will change the way art is

Educate Yourself

Start now by looking at art around you. Go to the local art museum and study the paintings, drawings, and sculptures. Take art classes at school or at the local recreation center. Go into an art gallery and ask questions (intelligent ones) about the works you see there. You don't have to be embarrassed about this. The dealers know that you can't buy anything now, but the good ones will educate you so that when you can buy something you'll come back to them.

sold. Most customers will still want to go into a gallery, see the actual piece, and talk with a dealer before making the decision to purchase it.

FOR MORE INFORMATION

ASSOCIATIONS

Art and Antique Dealers League of America
1040 Madison Avenue
New York, NY 10021
(212) 879-7558
Web site: http://www.artantiquedealersleague.org
Its Web site has a list of dealers by specialty.

Art Dealers Association of America (ADAA)
575 Madison Avenue
New York, NY 10022
(212) 940-8590
Web site: http://www.artdealers.org
A professional organization for art dealers, the ADAA "seeks to promote the highest standards of connoisseurship, scholarship and ethical practice within the profession," according to its Web site.

Fine Art Dealers Association
Web site: http://www.fada.com
The members of this organization are dedicated to promoting a high degree of professionalism. Their Web site has links to member galleries.

The National Art and Antiques Dealers Association of America
220 East 56th Street
New York, NY 10022
(212) 826-9707
Web site: http://www.naadaa.org
This association promotes ethical standards and protects the interests of collectors and sellers of art.

WEB SITES

Alex Wengraf, London

http://www.wengraf.com/dealer.htm

This site features an article that this dealer wrote for the *Antiques Trade Gazette* about ways to become a dealer.

Art Dealer Overview

http://www.iwon.com/home/careers/industry_profile/
0,15625,41,00.html

An overview of the job of art dealer, including a survey with quotes from art dealers about their work.

Artist's Survival Guide

http://www.lib.umd.edu/ART/guides/survive.html

A list for artists compiled by the University of Maryland library. It offers career guides, periodicals, Web sites, and organizations for those interested in art careers.

Careers in the Antiques Trade

http://artantiques.allinfo-about.com/weekly/features/careers.html

Gives advice on how to get started in the business.

Find a Career—Career Details

http://www.clickonmycareer.com/careerdetails.asp?ID=2811

An ad for a specific job in an art gallery that will give you a good idea of what to look for in such a position.

BOOKS

Careers in Art Galleries, Art Dealer. Research No. 38, Career Research Monographs. Chicago: The Institute for Research, 1999.
This book outlines the basics about working as an art dealer.

Grant, Daniel. *The Business of Being an Artist*. New York: Allworth Press, 1996.
This book is intended primarily for artists, but it has a good section on the relationship between artists and art galleries. Worth a read.

PERIODICALS

Art and Antiques

Web site: http://www.artantiquesmag.com

This magazine gives you an idea of what people are collecting in fine art.

Art in America

575 Broadway
New York, NY 10012

This magazine covers the art scene in New York and has good ideas about displaying art.

14

THEATRICAL PRESS AGENT

If you would love to be involved in theater but would rather leave the acting and producing to others, you might consider becoming a theatrical press agent. As good as a show may be on its own merits, it won't sell tickets unless the public knows it exists. That's where the press agent comes in. Theatrical press agents handle all of the publicity for a show, getting the word out to the public that a play or musical is opening on Broadway or will soon come to the community. Press agents are used in all sorts of shows, including Broadway, off-Broadway, regional, and local theaters.

Theatrical press agents create press kits, which are appealing packets of information about the show, and send them to local or national newspapers, magazines, TV stations, and radio stations. They prepare biographies of the show's stars, write press releases, arrange interviews, and deal with the media. Theatrical press agents do not operate on banker's hours. They must be available during business hours to schedule interviews and communicate with the media, but they must also be available to see shows and attend functions and events afterward, often on weekends.

Probably the most critical part of the job of a theatrical press agent is to have the right contacts in the media. If a press release written to announce the opening of the latest Broadway show ends up in a newspaper's sports department, chances are it will be thrown away. Theatrical press agents have to be familiar with all of the media outlets in town. That includes daily and weekly newspapers, magazines, and radio and TV stations. The press agent must find the person in charge of entertainment at each of these outlets. A press release that has a specific name attached to it is much more likely to be read than one addressed to "entertainment editor." The agent must know the audiences for the various radio and TV stations. The way a production is advertised on a rock station may be very different from the way it is advertised on a classical music station.

Theatrical press agents plan events and press conferences before a show starts running in order to get reviewers excited about the show. Agents might arrange for one of the show's stars to be interviewed by the newspaper or to appear on talk shows. They could hold a preview of the show for the press. They might have a photo session in a unique local area. Agents can send out press releases that emphasize an unusual episode about the making of the show, or that describe a heartwarming story about a member of the cast. A press agent must have a lot of creativity to think of new ways to interest the media or to do something that has never been done before.

One of the biggest jobs of the theatrical press agent is planning the opening night gala. The agent makes sure that all reviewers and critics are present. A pre-opening reception gives the agent a chance to hand out press kits with photos and information about the show that will help the reviewers complete their articles. The agent is also available to answer questions, to thank the reviewers for

Michael Greif *(center)*, the director of *Rent*, smiles for the press cameras as he arrives at the opening of the award-winning Broadway musical. It is the press agent's job to make sure the event is covered by the media.

coming, and to ensure that the reviewers get to their seats on time. Once the show starts, the agent leaves the reviewers alone.

Education and Training

There are no specific educational requirements for being a theatrical press agent, but an interest in the theater is essential. You can start now by going to the theater and participating in productions as a member of the stage crew, lighting team, or publicity department. Read the paper before the show opens to see what kind of publicity it gets, and read it afterward to see if the reviews are good.

Many theatrical press agents belong to the Association of Theatrical Press Agents and Managers, a trade union. To become eligible to join, an agent must apprentice for two years and take an exam. Members of the association get union-negotiated wages and follow certain work rules.

Salary

Salaries for press agents vary by the size and kind of production, the location, and the agent's experience. Press agents working in New York make around $1,500 per week.

Outlook

The field of theatrical arts is expected to grow faster than the average for other occupations. The success of many theaters will depend on the ability of the press agent to generate interest. In many respects, press agents will have more steady employment than actors.

Tips for Writing a Press Release

- Date the press release and mark it FOR IMMEDIATE RELEASE.
- Be concise. Try to get the information on one page. Many busy people won't look past the first sheet. Take out the fancy language.
- Use a hook. Start the release with something that will make the recipient want to read more. This could be a little-known fact about the show, an interesting personal quirk of one of the cast, or an anecdote about the writing of the show.
- Remember the Ws—who, what, where, when, and why. Boldface the important dates and times so they stand out.
- At the top of the page, put a contact name, phone number, fax number, and e-mail address.

FOR MORE INFORMATION

ASSOCIATIONS

Association of Theatrical Press Agents and Managers (ATPAM)
165 West 46th Street
New York, NY 10036
(212) 719-3666
Web site: http://www.atpam.com
The ATPAM is the union for theatrical professionals and provides resources, protection, and benefits to its members.

Public Relations Society of America (PRSA)
33 Irving Place
New York, NY 10003-2376
Web site: http://www.prsa.org
PRSA is a professional organization for public relations professionals.

WEB SITES

California State University
http://www.careers.csulb.edu/monographs/theatre.html
A short description of theater careers and the employment outlook.

How I Take Successful Publicity Photos
http://www.nytheatre-wire.com/fotart.htm
A professional photographer gives tips for taking publicity photos.

Press Release Writing Tips
http://www.press-release-writing.com
This site gives ideas for the content of press releases and ways to make them effective.

Theater
http://www.cas.okstate.edu/career/what_to_do/theater.html
A description of the job of theatrical press agent and some practical experiences for entering this profession.

There's a New Press Agent in Town!
http://www.oobr.com/ads/copy/botCRThin.html
An example of how a press agent might announce services to the public.

BOOKS

Goldberg, Jan. *Real People Working in Entertainment*. Lincolnwood, IL: NTC Publishing Group, 1999.
This book features interviews with dozens of people who work in the entertainment industry. In addition, basic information about salary, job details, and training requirements is mentioned.

Yale, David, and Ann Knudsen. *Publicity & Media Relations Checklists*. New York: McGraw-Hill, 1995.
This book is a very helpful way to learn about jobs in publicity.

Yaverbaum, Eric. *Public Relations Kit for Dummies*. New York: Hungry Minds, Inc., 2001.
Discusses how to organize and orchestrate PR from budgets, coordinate various media outlets, and tie into advertising and marketing campaigns.

PERIODICALS

American Theatre
355 Lexington Avenue
New York, NY 10017
Web site:
http://www.tcg.org/frames/am_theatre/fs_am_theatre.htm
This magazines promotes not-for-profit theaters; they're a good place to get a start.

GLOSSARY

annuity An annual payment.

bid-calling The job an auctioneer performs, raising prices as buyers accept them.

claim Money paid in accordance with an insurance policy.

close To bring a sales agreement to a finish.

commission A percentage of a sale that a salesperson earns for his or her work.

covenant A binding agreement.

development officer A person who raises money for a nonprofit organization.

expenditure Expenses accumulated from doing a particular job.

franchise A business that is authorized to operate as part of a larger corporation.

lobbyist A person who solicits members of a legislature for the purpose of influencing legislation.

multitask To juggle many jobs at one time.

nonprofit organization An organization that does not operate for commercial means.

open house A period of time during which a space that is for sale or rent is open to any and all potential buyers or renters to view.

policy A certificate of insurance.

press kit A packaged set of promotional materials, such as photographs and background information, for distribution to the press.

press release An announcement of an event, performance, or other newsworthy item that is issued to the press.

remainders Excess books whose sales have dropped off and that are usually sold at a discount.

wholesale The sale of goods in large quantities to a retailer.

INDEX

About the Author

Carolyn Gard is a former teacher and freelance writer who writes mainly for teenagers. In addition, she does research for members of the Colorado state legislature. She lives in Boulder, Colorado, where she enjoys hiking with her German shepherds.

Photo Credits

Cover, pp. 108, 109, 113, 119, 122–123 © Corbis; pp. 9, 11 © Matthew Borkoski/Index Stock; pp. 14, 50, 55, 58, 82, 85 © Index Stock; pp. 18, 21 © Tina Jordan/Reed Exposition; pp. 27, 31 © Julie Jacobson/AP/Wide World Photos; p. 41 © Charles Bennett/AP/Wide World Photos; pp. 36, 39 © Paul B. Southerland; pp. 45, 47 © Jon C. Hancock/AP/Wide World Photos; pp. 63, 65 © Douglas Healey/AP/Wide World Photos; p. 67 © Dario Lopez-Mills/AP/Wide World Photos; pp. 73, 76 © Eric Horan/Index Stock; p. 78 © Michael Keller/Index Stock; pp. 90, 92–93 © Michael Caulfield/AP/Wide World Photos; pp. 99, 103 © Stephen J. Boitano/AP/Wide World Photos; p. 101 © Doug Dreyer/AP/Wide World Photos; p. 120 © DaveCaulkin/AP/Wide World Photos; pp. 130, 133 © Reed Saxon/AP/Wide World Photos.

Series Design

Evelyn Horovicz

Layout

Nelson Sá